STITCH YOUR SIGN

The Ins and Outs of
EMBROIDERY
and ASTROLOGY

T0364014

Running Press
Hachette Book Group
1290 Avenue of the Americas, New York, NY 10104
www.runningpress.com
@Running_Press

First Edition: April 2018

Published by Running Press, an imprint of Perseus Books, LLC, a subsidiary of Hachette Book Group, Inc.

The publisher is not responsible for websites (or their content) that are not owned by the publisher.

ISBN: 978-0-7624-6392-3

Introduction to Embroidery

Embroidery is the ancient art of decorating fabric using a needle and thread.

It has a place in many cultures and histories, going as far back as the third century BC in China. Over time, embroidery's popularity has declined in many societies. In the past few years, however, many people have begun to place a higher value on all things local and independent, returning to their cultural roots, and embroidery has found its way back into favor. To me, embroidery is painting on fabric, and as someone who has never been particularly gifted with a brush, it is a rewarding way to express yourself, as well as an opportunity to meditate on the self and who you are at your core.

How

---- *to* ----

Stitch

Before we begin crafting our embroidered masterpieces, there are a few key stitches to learn.

The French Knot Stitch

Begin by bringing your thread up through the bottom side of the fabric, where you want your knot to be. With your hoop on a flat surface (or your lap!), pinch the floss about two inches above the fabric. Make sure to pinch the floss with your non-needle hand. Position your needle horizontally in front of the floss below where you're pinching the thread. Using your hand that is pinching the floss, wrap the thread around the needle between two and five times, depending on how big you want your knot to be (the more times you wrap the floss, the bigger the resulting knot). Once you've wrapped your floss around the needle—still pinching the thread with your non-dominant hand—pull the floss tight and push the needle back into the fabric next to your original hole, taking care not to pull the needle through the fabric just yet. Using your non-needle hand, which should still be tightly pinching

the floss, gently pull the floss
down the needle towards the
fabric. You should see the
floss bunch into a knot when
you do this. Once you see
the thread bunch, push the
needle the rest of the way
through the knot and pull it
all the way through. Once
your needle is pulled through,
repeat the knot anywhere else
the pattern calls for a dot.

Running Stitch

Insert your needle into the back of the fabric at one end of any line you want to stitch and push the needle through the front of the fabric a short distance away—for these patterns, the end of any star segment is a good distance.

Push your needle up through the back of the fabric at the start of the next line segment and repeat until all lines have been stitched.

How to Stitch Your Sign

Tape your fabric on top of the pattern for your zodiac sign. Holding the fabric up to a light source (like a window, or an iPad) trace the pattern onto the fabric using a pencil or piece of chalk. Once you've transferred the entire pattern to the fabric, remove the pattern from the fabric. It's very important to make sure the entire pattern has been transferred to the fabric, otherwise it will be difficult to transfer the missing pieces later. Next, take your hoop and loosen the screw at the top until you can separate the two rings. Place the fabric, with your pattern in the

center, on top of the inner
hoop and gently push the
outer hoop down, locking the
fabric in place between the
two hoops. Tighten the screw
as much as possible, securing
the fabric so it won't move.

Take your embroidery
floss, and separate two or
three strands out from the
rest (depending on how thick
you want your stiches to

be). Take the separated floss and wrap it around your forefinger, a quarter inch or so from the bottom of one end of the thread. Rub your thumb across your forefinger, rolling the thread around itself. Carefully slide the knot off your forefinger, leaving the twists intact, and pull on the thread on either side of the loop until it forms a knot.

Stitch all of the dots using the French knot stitch, described above. Then, stitch all of the lines using the running stitch, described above.

--- The ---
Signs

ARIES · *The Ram*

MARCH 21 – APRIL 19

Brave, Strong-Minded, Positive,
Honest, Impatient, Temperamental

TAURUS · *The Bull*

APRIL 20 – MAY 20

Dependable, Patient, Realistic, Steady,
Stubborn, Controlling, Rigid

GEMINI · *The Twins*

♊

MAY 21 – JUNE 21

Gentle, Warm, Inquisitive, Flexible,
Worried, Erratic, Hesitant

CANCER · *The Crab*

JUNE 22 – JULY 22

Persistent, Creative, Expressive,
Understanding, Temperamental,
Guarded, Insecure

LEO · *The Lion*

JULY 23 – AUGUST 22

Imaginative, Passionate, Warm, Jovial,
Overconfident, Obstinate, Selfish

VIRGO • *The Maiden*

AUGUST 23 – SEPTEMBER 22
Devoted, Logical, Diligent, Down-to-Earth, Wary, Concerned, Critical

LIBRA · *The Scales*

SEPTEMBER 23 – OCTOBER 22

Accommodating, Tactful,
Fair-Minded, Uncertain,
Non-Confrontational, Holds a Grudge

SCORPIO · *The Scorpion*

OCTOBER 23 – NOVEMBER 21

Inventive, Valiant, Impassioned,
Stubborn, Cynical, Guarded

SAGITTARIUS · *The Archer*

NOVEMBER 22 – DECEMBER 21

Generous, Principled, Funny,
Overpromises, Irritable, Tactless

CAPRICORN · *The Mountain Sea-Goat*

DECEMBER 22 – JANUARY 19

Dependable, Restrained, Serious,
Condescending, Exacting, Egotistical

AQUARIUS *The Water-Bearer*

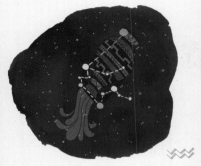

JANUARY 20 – FEBRUARY 18

Open-Minded, Creative, Independent,
Guarded, Detached, Inflexible

PISCES · *The Fish*

FEBRUARY 19 – MARCH 20

Empathetic, Creative, Tender,
Fearful, Naïve, Gloomy

This book has been bound using handcraft methods and Smyth-sewn to ensure durability.

The text was written by Anna Fleiss.

The cover and interior were illustrated by Mara Penny and designed by Ashley Todd.